W9-AVC-732

Pebble Bilingual Books

La luz del sol/
Sunshine

de/by
Gail Saunders-Smith

ISCARD

Traducción/Translation
Martín Luis Guzmán Ferrer, Ph.D.

Capstone Press
Mankato, Minnesota

Public Library, New Brunswick, NJ

Pebble Bilingual Books are published by Capstone Press
151 Good Counsel Drive, P.O. Box 669, Mankato, Minnesota 56002
http://www.capstone-press.com

Copyright © 2004 by Capstone Press. All rights reserved.
No part of this publication may be reproduced in whole or in part, or stored in a
retrieval system, or transmitted in any form or by any means, electronic, mechanical,
photocopying, recording, or otherwise, without written permission of the publisher.
For information regarding permission, write to Capstone Press,
151 Good Counsel Drive, P.O. Box 669, Dept. R, Mankato, Minnesota 56002.
Printed in the United States of America

1 2 3 4 5 6 08 07 06 05 04 03

Library of Congress Cataloging-in-Publication Data
Saunders-Smith, Gail.
    [Sunshine. Spanish & English]
    La luz del sol / de Gail Saunders-Smith; traducción, Martín Luis Guzmán
Ferrer = Sunshine / by Gail Saunders-Smith; translation, Martín Luis Guzmán Ferrer.
    p. cm.—(Pebble Bilingual Books)
    English and Spanish.
    Includes index.
    Summary: Describes the effects of light from the sun on earth and how it causes
temperature changes, the seasons, winds, and clouds.
    ISBN 0-7368-2310-7 (hardcover)
    1. Sunshine—Juvenile literature. 2. Weather—Juvenile literature. [1. Sunshine. 2.
Spanish language materials—Bilingual.] I. Title: Sunshine. II. Guzmán Ferrer, Martín
Luis. III. Title. IV. Series.
QC911.2.S2818 2004
551.5′271--dc21   2003004021

Editorial Credits
Martha E. H. Rustad, editor; Timothy Halldin, cover designer; Patrick Dentinger,
    interior designer and cover production designer; Michelle L. Norstad, photo
    researcher; Eida Del Risco, Spanish copy editor

Photo Credits
Cheryl R. Richter, 6; Chuck Place, 1, 4; International Stock/Ronn Maratea, 12; Photo
    Network International/Nancy Hoyt Belcher, 10; Richard Hamilton Smith, cover,
    14, 20; Unicorn Stock Photos/Jeff Greenberg, 16; William B. Folsom, 18; William
    Muñoz, 8

Special thanks to Ken Barlow, chief meteorologist, KARE-TV, Minneapolis,
Minnesota, and member of the American Meteorological Society, for his help in
preparing the English content of this book.

Table of Contents

Contenido

4

Sunshine is light from the sun.
Sunshine gives the earth light and
heat. Sunshine also makes weather
on the earth.

La luz solar es la luz que viene
del sol. La luz solar da luz y
calor a la Tierra. La luz solar
también forma el clima de
la Tierra.

Light from the sun travels to the earth in rays. The rays heat the atmosphere. Atmosphere is the air around the earth.

La luz del sol llega a la Tierra a través de rayos. Los rayos solares calientan la atmósfera. La atmósfera es el aire que rodea a la Tierra.

Sunshine falls on one-half of the earth at a time. It is day on one side of the earth. It is night on the other side. The earth spins. It moves places into and out of the light.

La luz del sol ilumina una mitad de la Tierra a la vez. Es de día en un lado de la Tierra. Es de noche en el otro lado. La Tierra gira. Así va metiendo y sacando de la luz todas sus zonas.

Galapagos Island, Ecuador

The equator is halfway between the top and the bottom of the earth. Sunshine is strongest at places near the equator. At noon, the sun is straight up in the sky. Sunshine makes the air very hot at the equator.

El ecuador divide a la Tierra por la mitad. La luz solar es más fuerte en los lugares cercanos al ecuador. Al mediodía el sol se encuentra en el cielo directamente hacia arriba. La luz solar hace que el aire sea muy caliente en el ecuador.

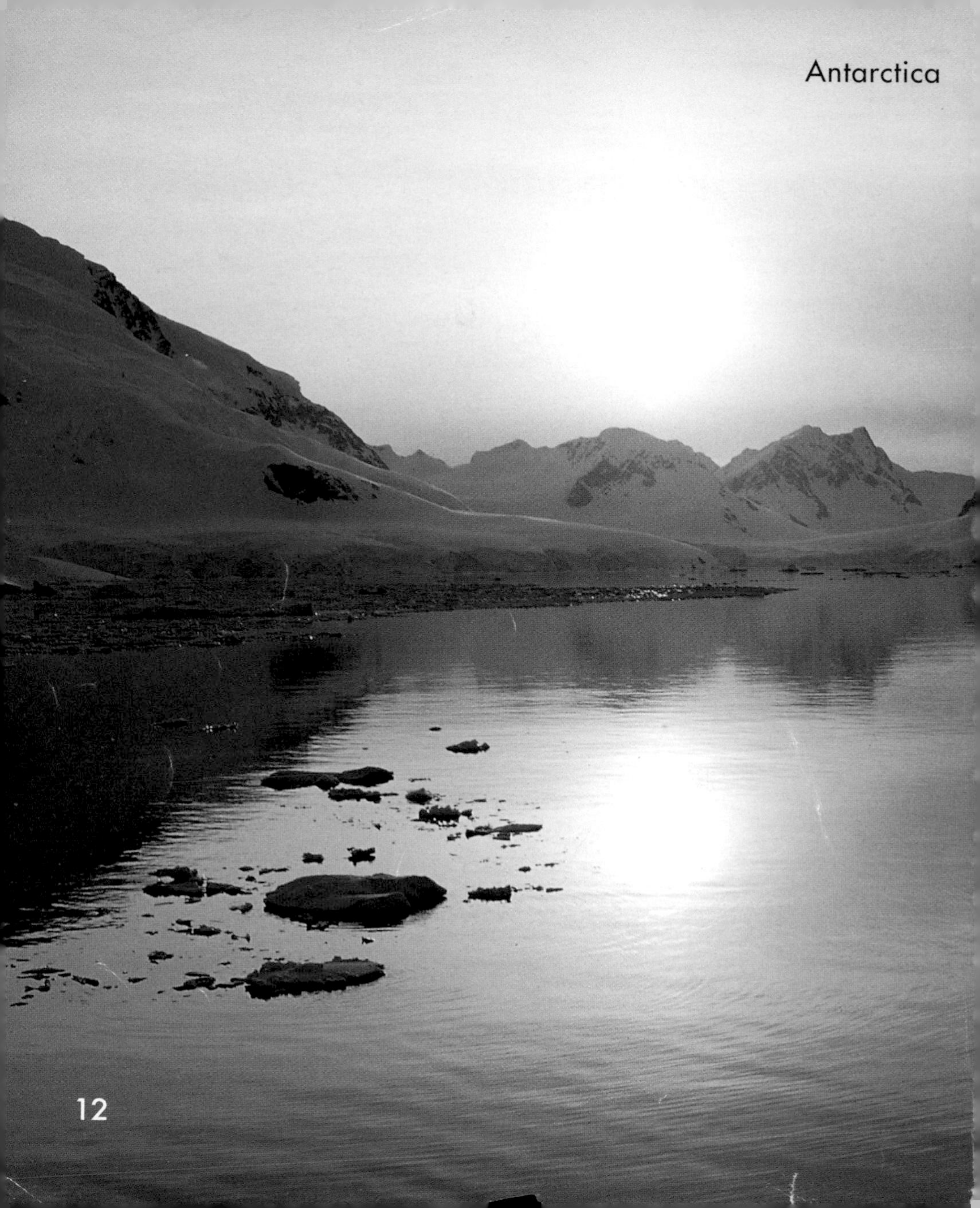
Antarctica

Sunshine is weaker at places near the top and the bottom of the earth. The sun does not go up very high in the sky. Sunshine does not heat the air as much. These places have ice and snow all year long.

La luz solar es débil en los lugares más alejados del ecuador. En esos lugares el sol no sube muy alto en el cielo. La luz solar no calienta mucho el aire. Esos lugares tienen hielo y nieve todo el año.

Sunshine makes the seasons. In June, the top of the earth points toward the sun. More sunshine hits the top half of the earth. It is summer here. Less sunshine hits the bottom half of the earth. It is winter there.

La luz solar forma las estaciones. En junio, la parte de arriba de la Tierra apunta directamente al sol. La parte de arriba de la Tierra recibe mucha luz solar. Ahí es verano. Pero la parte de abajo de la Tierra recibe mucha menos luz solar. Ahí es invierno.

15

In December, the top of the earth points away from the sun. Less sunshine hits the top half of the earth. It is winter here. More sunshine hits the bottom half of the earth. It is summer there.

En diciembre, la parte de arriba de la Tierra apunta en dirección opuesta al sol. La parte de arriba de la Tierra recibe menos luz solar. Ahí es invierno. Pero la parte de abajo recibe mucha mas luz solar. Ahí es verano.

18

Sunshine heats the atmosphere.
The rays of the sun heat some
places more than others. This
causes pockets of colder air and
pockets of warmer air. These
air pockets move and make wind.

La luz solar calienta la atmósfera.
Los rayos del sol calientan más
unos lugares que otros. Esto crea
bolsas de aire frío y bolsas de
aire caliente. Esas bolsas de aire
forman y mueven el viento.

Sunshine also heats bodies of water on the earth. The water evaporates. To evaporate means to go into the air. The water in the air gathers into clouds. The clouds carry water around the earth.

La luz solar también calienta las masas de agua de la Tierra. El agua se evapora. Evaporar significa elevarse en el aire. El agua en el aire forma las nubes. Las nubes llevan el agua alrededor de la Tierra.

Glossary

atmosphere—the air around the earth

equator—places on the earth that are halfway between the top and the bottom of the earth are on the equator

evaporate—when something wet goes into the air; when water evaporates, it turns into vapor.

season—one of the four parts of a year; spring, summer, autumn, and winter are the seasons.

weak—not strong

Glosario

atmósfera (la)—el aire que rodea la Tierra

ecuador (el)—línea que divide a la Tierra por la mitad

evaporarse—cuando algo mojado se eleva en el aire; cuando el agua se evapora se convierte en vapor.

estación (la)—cada una de las cuatro partes del año; primavera, verano, otoño e invierno son las estaciones.

débil—lo contrario de fuerte

Index

Índice